To Jim White —

May God Richly Bless You

GOD'S AWESOME HANDIWORK

GOD'S AWESOME HANDIWORK

FIRST EDITION

All Scriptures are from the King James Bible

ISBN 0-9769768-0-3

Alexander and Associates
532 Burbank Street
Williamsburg, Virginia 23185
757.784.3941

GOD'S AWESOME HANDIWORK

A COLLECTION OF SCRIPTURES AND TREES
THAT DISPLAY
GOD'S AWESOME HANDIWORK

HUBERT T. ALEXANDER SR.

INTRODUCTION

It is not often that you meet someone who has been endowed with great intellect and talent, who realizes that such gifts from God must be shared so that others may be blessed. To find someone willing to allow the gifts to enhance the lives of others is indeed a rare find, for unfortunately, ours is an age where many expect to be served rather than to serve. When I was asked to write the introduction to this book, I felt it a great honor to play a part in this divinely inspired endeavor. The choice of photographing trees in all their majesty and splendor makes one think of the God who created them. Joyce Kilmer wrote the immortal words, "Poems are made by fools like me but only God can make a tree."

Hubert Alexander and his proficiency with the camera has made unequivocally clear the words of Psalms 10:1, " The heavens declare the glory of God and the firmament sheweth his handiwork." Some of the oldest living things on earth are trees. Each is different, just as each snowflake and fingerprint are different. They stand proudly as sentinels of beauty.

I highly recommend this book for meditation to all who seek a quiet time with the Lord, for its pages are filled with the photographic mastery of the author and the stunning beauty of the book,_ *God's Awesome Handiwork.*

Rev. Dr. Solomon Wesley
Pastor (retired)
The Saint John Baptist Church
Williamsburg, Virginia

The fruit of the righteous is a tree of life, and he that winneth souls is wise.

"THE PURPOSE"

This book displays the awesome beauty of God's two great gifts to mankind. His Word, and his Works as displayed in his gift of trees. As you turn the pages, think of the reflective beauty of the scriptures and trees. Note how they complement each other - one to feed and replenish the physical soul, the other to replenish the physical self, to provide a wholesome environment, and to replenish the earth.

My prayer is that you are able to pick up this book, turn to any page and be uplifted as you ponder the unchanging word of God and awesome tree photography. It is recommended that the reader not try to read it as a connected book, but let each page stand alone to feed your needs for the moment: a pretty picture, an uplifting scripture or a time for reflection. Think of the awesome completeness as you study the tree's way of meeting Gods promise.

He will provide for your every need, as you await the return of his greatest gift as expressed in John 3:16 : For God so loved the world, that he gave his only begotten Son, that whosoever believeth in him should not perish, but have everlasting life.

DEDICATION

TO CATHERINE ALEXANDER, MY MOTHER

LISTON AND CATHERINE BURNS, MY IN-LAWS

BOBBYE ALEXANDER, MY WIFE OF 52 YEARS

HUBIE ALEXANDER, BELOVED SON

CATHERINE ALEXANDER, DAUGHTER

PEARL AND CHARLES INGS, DAUGHTER AND SON-IN-LAW

FLORA GALLIARD, SPECIAL FRIEND

JOHN AND EDNA HAYWOOD, MY CHEF AND FRIEND

GEORGE FAUREBACH, MY MENTOR

Hubert T. Alexander Sr.

ACKNOWLEDGMENTS

I wish to express special thanks to all who contributed to this book. To Bobbye and Catherine for believing in the project, and for their critical advice. To Dr. Jean Fenton for her enthusiastic critique and encouragement. To Carolyn Shirid, Lorie Smith and Fred Czufin for lending their artistic opinions. To Marian and Toby Lane for their technical support. To Dr. Solomon Wesley for his prayerful support and introduction. To Mrs. Nora Woodard for her encouragement.

I am blessed by your generous assistance

CONTENTS

Hebrews 13:5
Let your conversation be without covetousness; and be content with such things as
ye have: for he hath said, I will never leave thee, nor forsake thee.

PREFACE

My fascination with trees began as I grew up in tropical Florida surrounded by lush growth that included all kinds of fruit and flowering trees. The trees provided almost every need of a growing family/boy. I lived in a grove that included all varieties of citrus fruit, plus mangos, bananas, avocados, and guavas. When hungry, you reached out and grabbed something to eat. Or I hunted the prolific squirrels that lived in the trees and competed for the fruit. I emulated Tarzan by swinging from the vines that covered the trees. I carried wood from the forest to provide fuel for cooking and heat. The grove also included mama's "correction switch tree" that never had a shortage of switches used for correction and attention- getting purposes. I was also impressed by Mama's love for trees. She never failed to plant a tree given space and opportunity. I can still picture the stately oak trees, covered with Spanish moss and very colorful "flame vines". And I remember with great fondness, the trees that I, with my brothers cut down and hauled to the sawmill to be made into the lumber we used to build a home for Mama and the family.

Psalm 9:1
I will praise thee, O Lord, with my whole heart;
I will shew forth all thy marvelous works.

REFLECTIONS

We must continue to finds ways to experience the great goodness to mankind, in ways that are simply, colorful and enjoyable. We must find ways to appreciate the simple but great resources that God has made available to us. An all wise, loving caring God has made his presence and his love visible in so many ways.

John 3:16
For God so loved the world, that he gave his only begotten Son, that whosoever believeth in him should not perish, but have everlasting life.

Micah 6:8
He hath shewed thee, O man, what is good; and what doth the Lord require of thee, but to do justly, and to love mercy, and to walk humbly with thy God.

I hope this book will give you many reflective moments as you ponder God's word instructions and guidelines as given in the bible. The awesome beauty and utility as displayed in his tree kingdom. God has given his man creation so much, let us enjoy and appreciate it.

Isaiah 10:18-19
And shall consume the glory of his forest, and of his fruitful field, both soul and body: and they shall
be as when a standard bearer fainteth. And the rest of the trees of his forest shall be few,
that a child may write them.

1

Psalm 52:7-9
Lo, this is the man that made not God his strength; but trusted in the abundance of his riches,
and strengthened himself in his wickedness. [8] But I am like a green olive tree in the house of God:
I trust in the mercy of God for ever and ever. [9] I will praise thee for ever, because thou hast done it:
and I will wait on thy name; for it is good before thy saints.

Luke 17:6
And the Lord said, If ye had faith as a grain of mustard seed, ye might say unto this sycamine tree,
Be thou plucked up by the root, and be thou planted in the sea; and it should obey you.

Daniel 4:1-4
Nebuchadnezzar the king, unto all people, nations, and languages, that dwell in all the earth;
Peace be multiplied unto you. I thought it good to shew the signs and wonders that the high God
hath wrought toward me. How great are his signs! and how mighty are his wonders! his kingdom is
an everlasting kingdom, and his dominion is from generation to generation.

Genesis 1:11-12
And God said, Let the earth bring forth grass, the herb yielding seed, and the fruit tree yielding fruit after his kind, whose seed is in itself, upon the earth: and it was so. [12] And the earth brought forth grass, and herb yielding seed after his kind, and the tree yielding fruit, whose seed was in itself, after his kind: and God saw that it was good.

Isaiah 32:15
Until the spirit be poured upon us from on high, and the wilderness be a fruitful field,
and the fruitful field be counted for a forest.

Genesis 3:1-3
Now the serpent was more subtil than any beast of the field which the Lord God had made.
And he said unto the woman, Yea, hath God said, Ye shall not eat of every tree of the garden?
And the woman said unto the serpent, We may eat of the fruit of the trees of the garden:
But of the fruit of the tree which is in the midst of the garden, God hath said,
Ye shall not eat of it, neither shall ye touch it, lest ye die.

Psalm 50:10
For every beast of the forest is mine, and the cattle upon a thousand hills.

Genesis 2:9
And out of the ground made the Lord God to grow every tree that is pleasant to the sight, and
good for food; the tree of life also in the midst of the garden,
and the tree of knowledge of good and evil.

THE PROMISE

Psalm 23:1-6
A Psalm of David.
The Lord is my shepherd; I shall not want. He maketh me to lie down in green pastures: he leadeth me beside the still waters. He restoreth my soul: he leadeth me in the paths of righteousness for his name's sake. Yea, though I walk through the valley of the shadow of death, I will fear no evil: for thou art with me; thy rod and thy staff they comfort me. Thou preparest a table before me in the presence of mine enemies: thou anointest my head with oil; my cup runneth over Surely goodness and mercy shall follow me all the days of my life: and I will dwell in the house of the Lord for ever.

"IN YOUR MOMENT"

IN YOUR QUIET MOMENTS_____   "COMMUNICATE WITH HIM"

IN YOUR TROUBLED MOMENTS _____   "TRUST HIM"

IN YOUR HAPPY MOMENTS_____   "SHARE WITH HIM "

IN YOUR NEEDY MOMENTS _____   "ASK HIM"

IN YOUR GRATEFUL MOMENTS_____   "THANK HIM"

IN YOUR THOUGHTFUL MOMENTS_____   " COMMUNE WITH HIM"

IN YOUR LOST MOMENTS _____   "FIND HIM"

Proverbs 3:17-18
Her ways are ways of pleasantness, and all her paths are peace. [18] She is a tree of life to them that lay hold upon her: and happy is every one that retaineth her.

REMEMBER
"IF HE BROUGHT YOU TO THE SITUATION, HE WILL BRING YOU THROUGH IT"

Psalm 13:1-6
To the chief Musician, A
Psalm of David.
How long wilt thou forget
me, O Lord? For ever? How
long wilt thou hide thy face
from me? How long shall
I take counsel in my soul,
having sorrow in my heart
daily? How long shall mine
enemy be exalted over me?
Consider and hear me, O
Lord my God: lighten mine
eyes, lest I sleep the sleep of
death; Lest mine enemy say,
I have prevailed against him;
and those that trouble me
rejoice when I am moved.
But I have trusted in thy
mercy; my heart shall rejoice
in thy salvation. I will sing
unto the Lord, because he
hath dealt bountifully
with me.

Exodus 15:24-26
And the people murmured against Moses, saying, What shall we drink? And he cried unto
the Lord; and the Lord shewed him a tree, which when he had cast into the waters,
the waters were made sweet:

Psalm 19:1-14
To the chief Musician, A Psalm of David.

The heavens declare the glory of God; and the firmament sheweth his handywork. [2] Day unto day uttereth speech, and night unto night sheweth knowledge. [3] There is no speech nor language, where their voice is not heard. [4] Their line is gone out through all the earth, and their words to the end of the world. In them hath he set a tabernacle for the sun, [5] Which is as a bridegroom coming out of his chamber, and rejoiceth as a strong man to run a race. [6] His going forth is from the end of the heaven, and his circuit unto the ends of it: and there is nothing hid from the heat thereof. [7] The law of the Lord is perfect, converting the soul: the testimony of the Lord is sure, making wise the simple. [8] The statutes of the Lord are right, rejoicing the heart: the commandment of the Lord is pure, enlightening the eyes. [9] The fear of the Lord is clean, enduring for ever: the judgments of the Lord are true and righteous altogether. [10] More to be desired are they than gold, yea, than much fine gold: sweeter also than honey and the honeycomb. [11] Moreover by them is thy servant warned: and in keeping of them there is great reward. [12] Who can understand his errors? cleanse thou me from secret faults. [13] Keep back thy servant also from presumptuous sins; let them not have dominion over me: then shall I be upright, and I shall be innocent from the great transgression. [14] Let the words of my mouth, and the meditation of my heart, be acceptable in thy sight, O Lord, my strength, and my redeemer.

Psalm 92:12-14

The righteous shall flourish like the palm tree: he shall grow like a cedar in Lebanon. Those that be planted in the house of the Lord shall flourish in the courts of our God. They shall still bring forth fruit in old age; they shall be fat and flourishing;

"THE PALM TREE OF MY LIFE"

This palm tree stands within thirty feet from the spot where I was born over eighty years ago. This tree was ever present in my life as I learned the lessons of life from my Mother, as she struggled to raise eight children, to teach them the lessons of life and to instill in us her values of life and living and Her love for God and family. The lessons that have followed us throughout our lives.

THE TREE OF MY YOUTH"
Psalm 1:1-3

Blessed is the man that walketh not in the counsel of the ungodly, nor standeth in the way of sinners, nor sitteth in the seat of the scornful. But his delight is in the law of the Lord; and in his law doth he meditate day and night. And he shall be like a tree planted by the rivers of water, that bringeth forth his fruit in his season; his leaf also shall not wither; and whatsoever he doeth shall prosper.

This centuries-old camphor tree was the scene of many childhood
afternoon play sessions with the Miller children, Martha, Walter, Fannie Mae and Kenneth.
The lessons learned up and under this tree helped shape our lives
and to forge lifelong friendships

"THE TREE IN MY BACKYARD"
This Crepe Myrtle tree was planted by my Mother, Catherine Alexander on her first visit to our home in Williamsburg, Virginia over forty years ago.

Zech. 1:10-11
And the man that stood among the myrtle trees answered and said, These are they whom the Lord hath sent to walk to and fro through the earth. And they answered the angel of the Lord that stood among the myrtle trees, and said, We have walked to and fro through the earth, and, behold, all the earth sitteth still, and is at rest.

"THE CREATION"

Genesis 1:1-31

In the beginning God created the heaven and the earth. [2] And the earth was without form, and void; and darkness was upon the face of the deep. And the Spirit of God moved upon the face of the waters.

[3] And God said, Let there be light: and there was light. [4] And God saw the light, that it was good: and God divided the light from the darkness. [5] And God called the light Day, and the darkness he called Night. And the evening and the morning were the first day.

[6] And God said, Let there be a firmament in the midst of the waters, and let it divide the waters from the waters. [7] And God made the firmament, and divided the waters which were under the firmament from the waters which were above the firmament: and it was so. [8] And God called the firmament Heaven. And the evening and the morning were the second day.

[9] And God said, Let the waters under the heaven be gathered together unto one place, and let the dry land appear: and it was so. [10] And God called the dry land Earth; and the gathering together of the waters called he Seas: and God saw that it was good. [11] And God said, Let the earth bring forth grass, the herb yielding seed, and the fruit tree yielding fruit after his kind, whose seed is in itself, upon the earth: and it was so. [12] And the earth brought forth grass, and herb yielding seed after his kind, and the tree yielding fruit, whose seed was in itself, after his kind: and God saw that it was good. [13] And the evening and the morning were the third day.

[14] And God said, Let there be lights in the firmament of the heaven to divide the day from the night; and let them be for signs, and for seasons, and for days, and years: [15] And let them be for lights in the firmament of the heaven to give light upon the earth: and it was so. [16] And God made two great lights; the greater light to rule the day, and the lesser light to rule the night: he made the stars also. [17] And God set them in the firmament of the heaven to give light upon the earth, [18] And to rule over the day and over the night, and to divide the light from the darkness: and God saw that it was good. [19] And the evening and the morning were the fourth day. [20] And God said, Let the waters bring forth abundantly the moving creature that hath life, and fowl that may fly above the earth in the open firmament of heaven. [21] And God created great whales, and every living creature that moveth, which the waters brought forth abundantly, after their kind, and every winged fowl after his kind: and God saw that it was good. [22] And God blessed them, saying, Be fruitful, and multiply, and fill the waters in the seas, and let fowl multiply in the earth. [23] And the evening and the morning were the fifth day.

[24] And God said, Let the earth bring forth the living creature after his kind, cattle, and creeping thing, and beast of the earth after his kind: and it was so. [25] And God made the beast of the earth after his kind, and cattle after their kind, and every thing that creepeth upon the earth after his kind: and God saw that it was good.

[26] And God said, Let us make man in our image, after our likeness: and let them have dominion over the fish of the sea, and over the fowl of the air, and over the cattle, and over all the earth, and over every creeping thing that creepeth upon the earth. [27] So God created man in his own image, in the image of God created he him; male and female created he them. [28] And God blessed them, and God said unto them, Be fruitful, and multiply, and replenish the earth, and subdue it: and have dominion over the fish of the sea, and over the fowl of the air, and over every living thing that moveth upon the earth.

[29] And God said, Behold, I have given you every herb bearing seed, which is upon the face of all the earth, and every tree, in the which is the fruit of a tree yielding seed; to you it shall be for meat. [30] And to every beast of the earth, and to every fowl of the air, and to every thing that creepeth upon the earth, wherein there is life, I have given every green herb for meat: and it was so. [31] And God saw every thing that he had made, and, behold, it was very good. And the evening and the morning were the sixth day.

17

Isaiah 55:12
For ye shall go out with joy, and be led forth with peace: the mountains and the hills shall break forth before you into singing, and all the trees of the field shall clap their hands.

18

Ezekiel 31:6-8
All the fowls of heaven made their nests in his boughs, and under his branches did all the beasts of
the field bring forth their young, and under his shadow dwelt all great nations. Thus was he fair in
his greatness, in the length of his branches: for his root was by great waters. The cedars in the garden
of God could not hide him: the fir trees were not like his boughs, and the chesnut trees were not like
his branches; nor any tree in the garden of God was like unto him in his beauty.

Genesis 21:33
And Abraham planted a grove in Beer-sheba, and called there on the name of the Lord,
the everlasting God.

Matthew 3:10
And now also the axe is laid unto the root of the trees: therefore every tree which bringeth not forth good fruit is hewn down, and cast into the fire.

Genesis 1:11-13
And God said, Let the earth bring forth grass, the herb yielding seed, and the fruit tree yielding fruit after his kind, whose seed is in itself, upon the earth: and it was so. And the earth brought forth grass, and herb yielding seed after his kind, and the tree yielding fruit, whose seed was in itself, after his kind: and God saw that it was good. And the evening and the morning were the third day.

Psalm 96: 11-12

Let the heavens rejoice, and let the earth be glad; let the sea roar, and the fulness thereof.
Let the field be joyful, and all that is therein: then shall all the trees of the wood rejoice.

THE WORD

Psalm 1:1-6

Blessed is the man that walketh not in the counsel of the ungodly, nor standeth in the way of sinners, nor sitteth in the seat of the scornful. But his delight is in the law of the Lord; and in his law doth he meditate day and night. And he shall be like a tree planted by the rivers of water, that bringeth forth his fruit in his season; his leaf also shall not wither; and whatsoever he doeth shall prosper. The ungodly are not so: but are like the chaff which the wind driveth away. Therefore the ungodly shall not stand in the judgment, nor sinners in the congregation of the righteous. For the Lord knoweth the way of the righteous: but the way of the ungodly shall perish.

THE CREATOR'S

AWESOME

SUSTAINING

GIFTS

THE TREES

Genesis 2:7-9

And the Lord God formed man of the dust of the ground, and breathed into his nostrils the breath of life; and man became a living soul.

And the Lord God planted a garden eastward in Eden; and there he put the man whom he had formed.   And out of the ground made the Lord God to grow every tree that is pleasant to the sight, and good for food; the tree of life also in the midst of the garden, and the tree of knowledge of good and evil.

Rev. 22:2
In the midst of the street of it, and on either side of the river, was there the tree of life, which bare twelve manner of fruits, and yielded her fruit every month: and the leaves of the tree were for the healing of the nations.

Proverbs 3:17-18
Her ways are ways of pleasantness, and all her paths are peace. [18] She is a tree of life to them that lay hold upon her: and happy is every one that retaineth her.

Isaiah 55:11-13

So shall my word be that goeth forth out of my mouth: it shall not return unto me void, but it shall accomplish that which I please, and it shall prosper in the thing whereto I sent it. For ye shall go out with joy, and be led forth with peace: the mountains and the hills shall break forth before you into singing, and all the trees of the field shall clap their hands. Instead of the thorn shall come up the fir tree, and instead of the brier shall come up the myrtle tree: and it shall be to the Lord for a name, for an everlasting sign that shall not be cut off.

Neh. 10:35
And to bring the firstfruits of our ground, and the firstfruits of all fruit of all trees,
year by year, unto the house of the Lord:

Matthew 13:31-32
Another parable put he forth unto them, saying, The kingdom of heaven is like to a grain of mustard seed, which a man took, and sowed in his field: Which indeed is the least of all seeds: but when it is grown, it is the greatest among herbs, and becometh a tree, so that the birds of the air come and lodge in the branches thereof.

Psalm 1:1-6

Blessed is the man that walketh not in the counsel of the ungodly, nor standeth in the way of sinners, nor sitteth in the seat of the scornful. But his delight is in the law of the Lord; and in his law doth he meditate day and night. And he shall be like a tree planted by the rivers of water, that bringeth forth his fruit in his season; his leaf also shall not wither; and whatsoever he doeth shall prosper. The ungodly are not so: but are like the chaff which the wind driveth away. Therefore the ungodly shall not stand in the judgment, nor sinners in the congregation of the righteous. For the Lord knoweth the way of the righteous: but the way of the ungodly shall perish.

Genesis 1:11
And God said, Let the earth bring forth grass, the herb yielding seed, and the fruit tree yielding fruit after his kind, whose seed is in itself, upon the earth: and it was so.

Isaiah 44:23
Sing, O ye heavens; for the Lord hath done it: shout, ye lower parts of the earth: break forth
into singing, ye mountains, O forest, and every tree therein: for the Lord hath redeemed Jacob,
and glorified himself in Israel.

1 Kings 14:23
For they also built them high places, and images, and groves, on every high hill,
and under every green tree.

1 Kings 6:29
And he carved all the walls of the house round about with carved figures of cherubims and palm trees and open flowers, within and without.

Leviticus 26:3-4
If ye walk in my statutes, and keep my commandments, and do them; Then I will give you rain in due season, and the land shall yield her increase, and the trees of the field shall yield their fruit.

Ezekiel 47:7
Now when I had returned, behold, at the bank of the river were very many trees on the one side
and on the other.

Rev. 22:12-14

And, behold, I come quickly; and my reward is with me, to give every man according as his work shall be. [13] I am Alpha and Omega, the beginning and the end, the first and the last. [14] Blessed are they that do his commandments, that they may have right to the tree of life, and may enter in through the gates into the city.

Proverbs 13:12
Hope deferred maketh the heart sick: but when the desire cometh, it is a tree of life.

Rev. 22:14
Blessed are they that do his commandments, that they may have right to the tree of life, and may enter in through the gates into the city.

John 3:16
For God so loved the world, that he gave his only begotten Son, that whosoever believeth in him should not perish, but have everlasting life.

THE SILENT GUARDIAN

Genesis 1:11-15

And God said, Let the earth bring forth grass, the herb yielding seed, and the fruit tree yielding fruit after his kind, whose seed is in itself, upon the earth: and it was so. And the earth brought forth grass, and herb yielding seed after his kind, and the tree yielding fruit, whose seed was in itself, after his kind: and God saw that it was good. And the evening and the morning were the third day. And God said, Let there be lights in the firmament of the heaven to divide the day from the night; and let them be for signs, and for seasons, and for days, and years: And let them be for lights in the firmament of the heaven to give light upon the earth: and it was so. Since the third of day of creation, trees have stood as silent guardians watching over mankind, and silently recording history as it unfolded

THE EMANCIPATION OAK

Standing majestically on the campus of Hampton University is the "EMANCIPATION OAK." Tradition says that this is the scene of the first reading of the Emancipation Proclamation to former slaves from the south in 1863. On August 6, 1861 the confiscation Act of the Emancipation Proclamation was signed by President Abraham Lincoln and declared that all slaves of rebellious states would become chattel of the UnionArmy. The Emancipation Proclamation became the frame work for the Thirteenth Amendment to the Constitution. This amendment fortified the Emancipation Proclamation and prohibited slavery in all territories of the United States. According to history Mrs. Mary Peake the daughter of a freed slave woman and a Frenchman read the Emancipation Proclamation under the living branches of the live oak tree known today as the "Emancipation Oak" Tradition also believes that this is the beginning of formal education for freed slaves. In 1861 Mrs. Peak started a school for ex-slaves

John 12:13
Took branches of palm trees, and went forth to meet him, and cried, Hosanna:
Blessed is the King of Israel that cometh in the name of the Lord.

Ezekiel 31:8
The cedars in the garden of God could not hide him: the fir trees were not like his boughs, and the chesnut trees were not like his branches; nor any tree in the garden of God was like unto him in his beauty.

Isaiah 44:13-14

The carpenter stretcheth out his rule; he marketh it out with a line; he fitteth it with planes, and he marketh it out with the compass, and maketh it after the figure of a man, according to the beauty of a man; that it may remain in the house. He heweth him down cedars, and taketh the cypress and the oak, which he strengtheneth for himself among the trees of the forest: he planteth an ash, and the rain doth nourish it.

Psalm 96:11-12
Let the heavens rejoice, and let the earth be glad; let the sea roar, and the fulness thereof. Let the
field be joyful, and all that is therein: then shall all the trees of the wood rejoice

Psalm 104:15-16
And wine that maketh glad the heart of man, and oil to make his face to shine, and bread which strengtheneth man's heart. The trees of the Lord are full of sap; the cedars of Lebanon, which he hath planted;

Proverbs 3:17-18
Her ways are ways of pleasantness, and all her paths are peace. She is a tree of life to them that lay
hold upon her: and happy is every one that retaineth her.

Genesis 2:8-10
And the Lord God planted a garden eastward in Eden; and there he put the man whom he had formed. And out of the ground made the Lord God to grow every tree that is pleasant to the sight, and good for food; the tree of life also in the midst of the garden, and the tree of knowledge of good and evil. And a river went out of Eden to water the garden; and from thence it was parted, and became into four heads.

Psalm 61:1-8
To the chief Musician upon Neginah, A Psalm of David.

Hear my cry, O God; attend unto my prayer. [2] From the end of the earth will I cry unto thee, when my heart is overwhelmed: lead me to the rock that is higher than I. [3] For thou hast been a shelter for me, and a strong tower from the enemy. [4] I will abide in thy tabernacle for ever: I will trust in the covert of thy wings. Selah. [5] For thou, O God, hast heard my vows: thou hast given me the heritage of those that fear thy name. [6] Thou wilt prolong the king's life: and his years as many generations. [7] He shall abide before God for ever: O prepare mercy and truth, which may preserve him. [8] So will I sing praise unto thy name for ever, that I may daily perform my vows.

Psalm 23:1-6
A Psalm of David.

The Lord is my shepherd; I shall not want. He maketh me to lie down in green pastures: he leadeth me beside the still waters. He restoreth my soul: he leadeth me in the paths of righteousness for his name's sake. Yea, though I walk through the valley of the shadow of death, I will fear no evil: for thou art with me; thy rod and thy staff they comfort me. Thou preparest a table before me in the presence of mine enemies: thou anointest my head with oil; my cup runneth over. Surely goodness and mercy shall follow me all the days of my life: and I will dwell in the house of the Lord for ever.

Genesis 3:11-12
And he said, Who told thee that thou wast naked? Hast thou eaten of the tree, whereof I
commanded thee that thou shouldest not eat? And the man said, The woman whom thou gavest
to be with me, she gave me of the tree, and I did eat.

Genesis 3:3
But of the fruit of the tree which is in the midst of the garden, God hath said,
Ye shall not eat of it, neither shall ye touch it, lest ye die.

Proverbs 11:29-31
He that troubleth his own house shall inherit the wind: and the fool shall be servant to the wise of heart. The fruit of the righteous is a tree of life; and he that winneth souls is wise. Behold, the righteous shall be recompensed in the earth: Much more the wicked and the sinner.

Song 2:13
The fig tree putteth forth her green figs, and the vines with the tender grape give a good smell.
Arise, my love, my fair one, and come away.

THE HISTORY OF GOD'S TREE CREATION

GENESIS 1:13
AND THE EVENING AND THE MORNING WERE THE THIRD DAY.

HISTORICAL FACTS

THE WORLD'S OLDEST TREES ARE BRISTLECONE PINES IN THE USA.

THERE ARE 20,000 TYPES OF TREES GROWING AROUND THE WORLD.

A BRISTLECONE TREE NAMED "METHUSELAH" IN CALIFORNIA IS
MORE THAN 4,700 YEARS OLD.

THE TALLEST TREE IS AN AUSTRALIAN EUCALYPTUS ORIGINALLY
492 FEET TALL.

Matthew 21:19-21

And when he saw a fig tree in the way, he came to it, and found nothing thereon, but leaves only, and said unto it, Let no fruit grow on thee henceforward for ever. And presently the fig tree withered away. And when the disciples saw it, they marvelled, saying, How soon is the fig tree withered away! Jesus answered and said unto them, Verily I say unto you, If ye have faith, and doubt not, ye shall not only do this which is done to the fig tree, but also if ye shall say unto this mountain, Be thou removed, and be thou cast into the sea; it shall be done.

Matthew 24:31-33
And he shall send his angels with a great sound of a trumpet, and they shall gather together his elect from the four winds, from one end of heaven to the other. Now learn a parable of the fig tree; When his branch is yet tender, and putteth forth leaves, ye know that summer is nigh: So likewise ye, when ye shall see all these things, know that it is near, even at the doors.

Ezekiel 47:12
And by the river upon the bank thereof, on this side and on that side, shall grow all trees for meat, whose leaf shall not fade, neither shall the fruit thereof be consumed: it shall bring forth new fruit according to his months, because their waters they issued out of the sanctuary: and the fruit thereof shall be for meat, and the leaf thereof for medicine.

1 John 4:10
Herein is love, not that we loved God, but that he loved us, and sent his Son to be the
propitiation for our sins.

Leviticus 26:4 Leviticus 27:30

Then I will give you rain in due season, and the land shall yield her increase, and the trees of the field shall yield their fruit. And all the tithe of the land, whether of the seed of the land, or of the fruit of the tree, is the Lord's: it is holy unto the Lord.

Psalm 37:35
I have seen the wicked in great power, and spreading himself like a green bay tree.

Daniel 4:10-11
Thus were the visions of mine head in my bed; I saw, and behold a tree in the midst of the earth, and the height thereof was great. The tree grew, and was strong, and the height thereof reached unto heaven, and the sight thereof to the end of all the earth:

John 6:28-29
Then said they unto him, What shall we do, that we might work the works of God? Jesus answered and said unto them, This is the work of God, that ye believe on him whom he hath sent.

John 17:3
And this is life eternal, that they might know thee the only true God, and Jesus Christ,
whom thou hast sent.

Joel 1:18-20
How do the beasts groan! the herds of cattle are perplexed, because they have no pasture; yea, the flocks of sheep are made desolate. O Lord, to thee will I cry: for the fire hath devoured the pastures of the wilderness, and the flame hath burned all the trees of the field. The beasts of the field cry also unto thee: for the rivers of waters are dried up, and the fire hath devoured the pastures of the wilderness.

Neh. 9:25
And they took strong cities, and a fat land, and possessed houses full of all goods, wells digged,
vineyards, and oliveyards, and fruit trees in abundance: so they did eat, and were filled, and became
fat, and delighted themselves in thy great goodness.

Genesis 2:9
And out of the ground made the Lord God to grow every tree that is pleasant to the sight,
and good for food; the tree of life also in the midst of the garden, and the tree
of knowledge of good and evil.

2 Kings 3:19
And ye shall smite every fenced city, and every choice city, and shall fell every good tree, and stop all wells of water, and mar every good piece of land with stones.

1 Chron. 16:33
Then shall the trees of the wood sing out at the presence of the Lord,
because he cometh to judge the earth.

Neh. 10:35
And to bring the first fruits of our ground, and the first fruits of all fruit of all trees, year by year, unto the house of the Lord:

Genesis 3:3
But of the fruit of the tree which is in the midst of the garden, God hath said,
Ye shall not eat of it, neither shall ye touch it, lest ye die.

Rev. 2:7
He that hath an ear, let him hear what the Spirit saith unto the churches; To him that overcometh will I give to eat of the tree of life, which is in the midst of the paradise of God.

Psalm 1:3
And he shall be like a tree planted by the rivers of water, that bringeth forth his fruit in his
season; his leaf also shall not wither; and whatsoever he doeth shall prosper.

Psalm 52:8
But I am like a green olive tree in the house of God: I trust in the mercy of God for ever and ever.

Job 14:7
For there is hope of a tree, if it be cut down, that it will sprout again, and that the tender branch
thereof will not cease.

Genesis 21:33
And Abraham planted a grove in Beer-sheba, and called there on the name of the Lord, the everlasting God.

Daniel 4:10-11

Thus were the visions of mine head in my bed; I saw, and behold a tree in the midst of the earth, and the height thereof was great. The tree grew, and was strong, and the height thereof reached unto heaven, and the sight thereof to the end of all the earth:

Ezekiel 31:18
To whom art thou thus like in glory and in greatness among the trees of Eden? yet shalt thou be brought down with the trees of Eden unto the nether parts of the earth: thou shalt lie in the midst of the uncircumcised with them that be slain by the sword. This is Pharaoh and all his multitude, saith the Lord God.

Psalm 23:1-6
A Psalm of David.

The Lord is my shepherd; I shall not want. He maketh me to lie down in green pastures: he leadeth me beside the still waters. He restoreth my soul: he leadeth me in the paths of righteousness for his name's sake. Yea, though I walk through the valley of the shadow of death, I will fear no evil: for thou art with me; thy rod and thy staff they comfort me. Thou preparest a table before me in the presence of mine enemies: thou anointest my head with oil; my cup runneth over. Surely goodness and mercy shall follow me all the days of my life: and I will dwell in the house of the Lord for ever.

Genesis 2:8-9
And the Lord God planted a garden eastward in Eden; and there he put the man whom he had formed. And out of the ground made the Lord God to grow every tree that is pleasant to the sight, and good for food; the tree of life also in the midst of the garden, and the tree of knowledge of good and evil.

Psalm 8:1-9
To the chief Musician upon Gittith, A Psalm of David.
O Lord our Lord, how excellent is thy name in all the earth! who hast set thy glory above the
heavens. Out of the mouth of babes and sucklings hast thou ordained strength because of thine
enemies, that thou mightest still the enemy and the avenger. When I consider thy heavens, the
work of thy fingers, the moon and the stars, which thou hast ordained; What is man, that thou art
mindful of him? and the son of man, that thou visitest him? For thou hast made him a little lower
than the angels, and hast crowned him with glory and honour. Thou madest him to have dominion
over the works of thy hands; thou hast put all things under his feet: All sheep and oxen, yea, and the
beasts of the field; The fowl of the air, and the fish of the sea, and whatsoever passeth through the
paths of the seas. O Lord our Lord, how excellent is thy name in all the earth!

81

Psalm 8:1-9
To the chief Musician upon Gittith, A Psalm of David.
O Lord our Lord, how excellent is thy name in all the earth! who hast set thy glory above the heavens. Out of the mouth of babes and sucklings hast thou ordained strength because of thine enemies, that thou mightest still the enemy and the avenger. When I consider thy heavens, the work of thy fingers, the moon and the stars, which thou hast ordained; [4] What is man, that thou art mindful of him? and the son of man, that thou visitest him? For thou hast made him a little lower than the angels, and hast crowned him with glory and honour. Thou madest him to have dominion over the works of thy hands; thou hast put all things under his feet:] All sheep and oxen, yea, and the beasts of the field; The fowl of the air, and the fish of the sea, and whatsoever passeth through the paths of the seas. O Lord our Lord, how excellent is thy name in all the earth!

Luke 3:9
And now also the axe is laid unto the root of the trees: every tree therefore which bringeth
not forth good fruit is hewn down, and cast into the fire.

Job 14:8-10
Though the root thereof wax old in the earth, and the stock thereof die in the ground; Yet
through the scent of water it will bud, and bring forth boughs like a plant. But man dieth, and
wasteth away: yea, man giveth up the ghost, and where is he?

Job 40:21-22
He lieth under the shady trees, in the covert of the reed, and fens.
The shady trees cover him with their shadow; the willows of the brook compass him about.

Ezekiel 31:14-16

To the end that none of all the trees by the waters exalt themselves for their height, neither shoot up their top among the thick boughs, neither their trees stand up in their height, all that drink water: for they are all delivered unto death, to the nether parts of the earth, in the midst of the children of men, with them that go down to the pit. Thus saith the Lord God; In the day when he went down to the grave I caused a mourning: I covered the deep for him, and I restrained the floods thereof, and the great waters were stayed: and I caused Lebanon to mourn for him, and all the trees of the field fainted for him. I made the nations to shake at the sound of his fall, when I cast him down to hell with them that descend into the pit: and all the trees of Eden, the choice and best of Lebanon, all that drink water, shall be comforted in the nether parts of the earth.

John 12:23-25
And Jesus answered them, saying, The hour is come, that the Son of man should be glorified. Verily, verily, I say unto you, Except a corn of wheat fall into the ground and die, it abideth alone: but if it die, it bringeth forth much fruit. He that loveth his life shall lose it; and he that hateth his life in this world shall keep it unto life eternal.

James 3:11-12
Doth a fountain send forth at the same place sweet water and bitter? Can the fig tree, my
brethren, bear olive berries? Either a vine, figs? So can no fountain both yield salt water and fresh.

Neh. 2:7-8

Moreover I said unto the king, If it please the king, let letters be given me to the governors beyond the river, that they may convey me over till I come into Judah; And a letter unto Asaph the keeper of the king's forest, that he may give me timber to make beams for the gates of the palace which appertained to the house, and for the wall of the city, and for the house that I shall enter into. And the king granted me, according to the good hand of my God upon me.

Genesis 3:6
And when the woman saw that the tree was good for food, and that it was pleasant to the eyes,
and a tree to be desired to make one wise, she took of the fruit thereof, and did eat, and gave also
unto her husband with her; and he did eat.

Genesis 3:17
And unto Adam he said, Because thou hast hearkened unto the voice of thy wife,
and hast eaten of the tree, of which I commanded thee, saying,
Thou shalt not eat of it: cursed is the ground for thy sake; in sorrow
shalt thou eat of it all the days of thy life;

Isaiah 44:22-23
I have blotted out, as a thick cloud, thy transgressions, and, as a cloud, thy sins: return unto me;
for I have redeemed thee. Sing, O ye heavens; for the Lord hath done it: shout, ye lower parts of
the earth: break forth into singing, ye mountains, O forest, and every tree therein: for the Lord hath
redeemed Jacob, and glorified himself in Israel.

Psalm 50:8-10
I will not reprove thee for thy sacrifices or thy burnt offerings, to have been continually before me.
I will take no bullock out of thy house, nor he goats out of thy folds. For every beast of the forest is
mine, and the cattle upon a thousand hills.

Isaiah 9:18- Isaiah 10:18-19
For wickedness burneth as the fire: it shall devour the briers and thorns, and shall kindle in the
thickets of the forest, and they shall mount up like the lifting up of smoke.
And shall consume the glory of his forest, and of his fruitful field, both soul and body: and they
shall be as when a standard-bearer fainteth. And the rest of the trees of his forest shall be few,
that a child may write them.

Ezekiel 15:6
Therefore thus saith the Lord God; As the vine tree among the trees of the forest,
which I have given to the fire for fuel, so will I give the inhabitants of Jerusalem.

Zech. 11:2
Howl, fir tree; for the cedar is fallen; because the mighty are spoiled: howl, O ye oaks of Bashan;
for the forest of the vintage is come down.

Rev. 22:12 Rev. 22:15
And, behold, I come quickly; and my reward is with me, to give every man according as his work
shall be. I am Alpha and Omega, the beginning and the end, the first and the last. Blessed are they
that do his commandments, that they may have right to the tree of life, and may
enter in through the gates into the city.

APPENDIX OF SCRIPTURES IN
GOD'S AWESOME HANDIWORK

Luke 11:28 But he said, Yea rather, blessed are they that hear the word of God, and keep it.

PSALM 52:8
BUT I AM LIKE A GREEN OLIVE TREE IN THE HOUSE OF GOD: I TRUST IN THE MERCY OF GOD FOR EVER AND EVER.